Woodland creature

Athena Wadey

BookLeaf Publishing

Presentation by *BookLeaf Publishing*

Web: www.bookleafpub.com

E-mail: info@bookleafpub.com

ISBN: 978-93-95755-53-5

First edition 2022

To the girls, gays and theys: you have made my life into a sweeter story.

PREFACE

In April 2020 I started writing poetry as a way to cope with the boredom and isolation of lockdown. Words started spilling out and they haven't since. Writing has become my way of savouring the joys of life and making sense of the darker moments. Through sharing my writing, I have realised that poetry connects me to others in a way I could never imagine. I hope somewhere in this book you find a passage or poem that makes you feel understood.

Love Athena x

delicate

I want to be delicate
A silk-laden babe
Mesmerising you
With her heavenly gaze

I want to be laid
On a field among daisies
Bathing in the midday sun

To be swathed in white linen
And gasping at the air
Clutching at the grass
My hair lain undone

I want to escape from this body that binds me
To the fate of silent suffering
From the chains that confine me

To breathe in that sweet nostalgia
Of a youth ever-wasted
Dreaming away days
Of the moonlights memories
Fabricated

I want to adorn myself in illustrations
Images of where i'm going

And where i've been

I want to be delicate
I want to be fair
The ethereal girl
With the sunlit hair

I am calloused and scarred
My cracks poorly filled
With sugar-coated words
And too many prescription pills

I tower above you
Alone in the sky
Gazing through the clouds
Wishing I could fly

I dream of a body
One that's not mine
A body that's petite
And delicate and fine

beachside

It's peculiar how
Colours seem brighter somehow
As if those metaphorical clouds
Weren't so metaphorical
When you ripped them away
And brought an aqua blue sky
Illuminating the world
In a transcendent light

I walk through a city
Of lights and old faces
Wedged together
Are the assortment of places
Where so many things
Have happened to me
To shape my life's purpose
My soul and entirety

I was born on a Monday, near the end of the
century
A coastal girl through and through
Ocean air wafting in
As I took my first breaths
At the height of an Australian summer

I never belonged in this world
Unable to bathe under the searing sun
The darkened, cold indoors
Are where I hosted all my fun
Of solitude and dreams of a life far away

I detested the ocean
Perhaps its beauty intimidated me
Or made me fear, that I was unworthy
Of the treasures that the earth has gifted us

Reluctant to open myself up
To the world and the elements
Debilitated and fearful
As if the sand
Would devour me whole
And spit me back out again

Do you remember when we used to play among
the trees?
I can still hear the sound of your old rusted
swing set
And smell that mid-afternoon breeze
When we would lay out your Mum's banana
lounge on the grass
And pretend it was a boat
I don't know where we were going
And I didn't ten years later

When I took a plane somewhere old
A land woven from memories
Another place and time
The birthplace of my father's childhood stories
Holding a sacred place in my heart and mind

This town has seen the best and the worst of me
The sleepless nights
And sordid love affairs
Between me and an unassuming suitor
To abandon upon sunrise

I have stumbled in a drunken haze
Along the streets of this city
Under the blinking streetlights
Arm in arm with the ones I love

I find it sad how some of the most important
people drift away
And you see them months later
On the dancefloor of a club
Both exclaiming that you must catch up soon
But neither of you really mean it

People fade into obscurity to let better people in
Full of stardust and moonlight
Finding their way under my skin

It happened slowly

And then it happened all at once
That the ocean, this town
Became a part of my blood

I had a dream a few nights ago
Of the first house that I called home
I awoke
And in my heart
There was only love.

thoughts from my bed

I woke up today
And the world was dying
So I combed my hair
And put on my lipstick and perfume

-

There I go again
Lying in my bed
Comparing myself
To a girl i've never met

But maybe
Just perhaps
In the outskirts of my reality
There's a girl out there
Lying in her bed
Wishing she was me

-

Perhaps I cannot write happy poetry
Because when life is good
I am too busy living it
To sit down and document

But when I am low
There is all the time in the world
To put pen to paper
And let the thoughts unfurl.

time to go

I will go when the universe tells me
When my skin is wrinkled
And every smile has been shone
Under every sky and moon

When the seeds of my soul
Have sprouted into flourishing gardens
That cover the plains of my life

When I have loved with every essence of my
being
Given everything to the cause
And my friends and family

When I have swum through every ocean
And savoured every summertime
When the breeze comes in
And the kookaburras sing their song
Before the rain falls

When I have learnt all the lessons
And waded through countless pitfalls
That I cannot fathom now

To become the strongest version

Of the woman I will ever be
Who is loud and strong
Ferocious and free
Of every doubt and cruelty that lie
Deep inside of me

I will go when the stars and the planets,
and the moon align
When I have reached almost a century
Aging like fine wine

When the ones I love
The ones that have gone
Come up close to my ear
And whisper softly
"it's time"

fairy lights

Since lockdown two
Things just haven't been the same
Like my friends and I
We look at each other and there's nothing to say

And ironically the more I stayed inside,
The less my house felt like home
And my only solace, once a day, was a
thirty-minute walk up and down the road

I believe there is a part of us still
That is sitting on the edge of our seats
Waiting for disaster to arise
Even when you are sitting contently
I can see it there in the back of your eyes

For me, pleasure and excitement are a distant
memory
I'm eating way too much takeaway
And I'm no longer drinking all that herbal tea

Clothes don't fit like they used to
And it's not that I'm more fat, or more thin
It's just that I don't feel the same as I did
Deep down within

Golds and deeps maroons
Seem like a cheap façade
When getting out of bed in the morning
Seems like the hardest task

Music and poetry don't move me like they used
to
With notes and pretty phrases
That send a shiver down my spine
That sparkle on my skin
Make the dingiest city sublime

To date or fall in love is the furthest thing from
my mind
I can't even leave the house anymore
I've completely stopped drinking wine

My ocean blues have turned to greys
And disappointingly
Unenthralled by wonderous change
I wander aimlessly alone
In a melancholy haze

Staring at bright lights
And my eyes glaze over
I look back to when the easiest way to excite me
Was a set of fairy lights
Wrapped around a swaying tree

And there I'd stand, drunk and eighteen
Staring at the glistening leaves
Moving in the breeze
And I don't know why
But it would make me feel free
Like anything could happen
Like my life was a growing tapestry
Of endless possibilities

I haven't called my parents, my family or my
friends
The people who used to be right there
When I needed help to mend
I don't know why, maybe I'm ashamed
Or maybe I like playing pretend
That everything is perfect
Exactly how I planned

Perhaps I'm just waiting for the day
When the colours decide to return
In a luminous cascade
And the blues, reds and greens
Will come out to play
And I'll sit on the bus
As it drives over the lake
Listening to a song
That feels like someone running their fingertips
Down my shoulders and back.

thoughts from the dicey's beer garden

I came back from home today
And I feel reborn
Like my mind and soul
Are finally making their way back home

I swear I drank cider for twelve hours straight
Until the barman kicked us out
I hadn't even realised it was late
And we sat on the curb at 4am
Eating hot chips

We sat in the beer garden and I thought
'My god this is it'
My reason to hold on
My reason to live

I looked at you both
Two of the best souls I've ever known
And realised it had been an age
Since my heart-beat had run so slow
Wherever you are,
That is my home

The air smells sweeter

Even when you're not as close to the sea
And I can feel happy memories
Brushing past my nose and cheeks
Dancing in the autumn breeze

There's something different about the way
The sun hits the buildings in the middle of the
day
Like the bricks are coated in gold
And the windows are made of cellophane

I'll get through this pain
Because I know that you'll be there waiting for
me
In that sparkly city by the sea
Full of beautiful, patchwork people
And that stupid floating palm tree

revolution

I welcome you all here tonight
To celebrate the strange
The queer
The untameable

Let me tell you a story
Of pain and loss
A modern day fairytale fable

Like all that are wrong
I have lived a life of contest
Of boat-rocking and rule-breaking
Of cultural and structural conquest

I refuse to celebrate mediocrity
Because I know how brave, how painful it is
To live as extraordinary

I am broken and blue
Tentatively pieced back together
Like jagged shards of glass
Lined carefully with PVA glue

I am furious, scared, unabashedly angry
How being true and without cruelty

Can be rare, borderline revolutionary

And this integrity I cling to at the loss of all else
Doing what is right, what must be done
Regardless of the cost to my health

Because the strongest I will ever be
Is when I am stripped to the barest state of
vulnerability
And I wear my heart on display
Bleeding and beating for all to see

For me, lights and sounds blare at a
high-frequency
And in my heart I have always felt that my
greatest weakness
Was my soul-encompassing sensitivity

But to live without shields is my greatest
accomplishment
The sadness is unbearable
But the happiness is just as strong
And there are moments when my life feels better
than
The sound of my favourite song
The moments of resistance, the moments of fear
Are what refine my soul
Build strength and spread love
Through my skin and into my bones

I know that this pain will somehow fade
And that these endless days
Will be the plot-points of a winding story
I tell someday

To be wrong is to be true
Sometimes battered and a little bruised
But my faith will never waver
My shields will never rise

Because my life is a revolution
And my revolution is love

Sunday sesh

we sit outside on a Sunday night
smoking vapes and sipping gin
talking shit about the boys we've seen
the books we're reading
the places we have and haven't been

our hair is perfectly tousled
and our jeans were bought at vinnies
we talk effortlessly about war and politics
powered on hot chips and cider tinnies

I confess that I worry i'll never fall in love
as I place my empty schooner on the bench
I'm just too broken
and I burn bridges quicker than a bushfire
rushing through gum trees and forest

she looks at me and lights a cigarette
she says she doesn't need a boyfriend
because she has a toy with a head that spins
sex is better when it's with someone you love
that's why it's better when it's just her

we look at the empty seat beside her

I say it hasn't been the same since she shacked
up
she hasn't been around and hasn't talked much
this happens all the time when your friends find
love

we tell the same story every week
telling ourselves it's changing
insert name here just doesn't understand
does he really care about me?
it feels like i'm dating a child
not a twenty three year old man

we're raging feminists
trying to make happenstance out of strategy
willing to fill the gap between what we desire
and what we can find

it's easy to have everything
but impossible to find someone who can see it

and perhaps I sabotage my chances
because all i'd rather be doing is sitting on a
wine stained couch
talking to you
about your failed dates
and all the things you're going through
because that's what real love is

the secret they don't tell us is that
we could put on our makeup and walk into every
bar in town
but we could never find anything better than
each other

1:30am

It's 1:30am and I haven't been to sleep yet
Because my jaw is aching
And life is still unfair
My heart has been beating out of my chest
Since I woke up this morning
At quarter past ten

I didn't go to work today
Because I couldn't keep my eyes open
And my body was too heavy to lift out of bed
Like I had gained the weight of the world
overnight

I bought soft pillows
And I filled the living room with old trinkets
Because this apartment doesn't feel like home

It's been six months and I haven't hooked up the
tv
Because I can't believe that this place is
anything but temporary
Although I have to admit to myself
That my old home has faded into eternity

At least I can walk into town where the cafes are
heaving
To sit in an empty corner to drink tea in
Attempting to solve all my problems with poetry

I'm sinking into that old habit
Where i'm dreaming away the day
I miss you so much
And life is so much simpler when you are here

But anyway I went to Target
And bought containers to organise my bathroom
cabinet
And maybe that will solve my life

human

In my past life
I was so rigid
Pious, judgemental
Undoubtedly religious

Unsubstantiated concerns
Still dwell inside of me
Among human desires
That make me feel obscene

I know for a fact
This is not my first trip
I knew it way back
Even when I was a little kid

It's like I aged backwards
Like a regular Benjamin Button
A hooligan, a youngin'
A typical ragamuffin

I feel younger now
Than I ever did
Making ill-informed decisions
Throwing caution into the wind
I was not birthed to be perfect

I was birthed to be real
To seek desires and love
To allow myself to feel

yellagong st

Store-bought olives
Autumn air
Only the restful wander here
Among the decaying trees
Their branches reaching out toward the sky
Leaves ebbing slowly
Toward the ground
Under the command of the afternoon breeze

Driving up the winding road with trepidation
The mountain that stood alongside me
In the journey of my life's creation

There is a silence that lies in the cracks
Between the trees
Where the sun shines through
Glistening at her peak at evening
upon five o'clock in the afternoon

A silence that it is not eerie or fearful
It welcomes me
Slithering through the moss that grows
Through the crevices on the back verandah
Tickling my feet as I upon it
One foot in front of the other

Towards the sun
That sits perched above the ocean line
Right over there in the distance

A stack sitting on the edge of the world
Billowing out smoke
That floated above the far away houses
Dotted along the horizon
At night shimmering in a cascade
Of blurry lights

Cockatoos would preen
And conjugate in a party of sorts
On the crumbling staircase that
Clung to the side of my room
The place that hosted all of the parties
And stories and games
That my imagination could conjure

There is a video I have watched
Of when I was small
Consisting of all the people that loved me
Even before the day I was born
We gathered around
A box full of souvenirs
Tokens to tell the story
Of what it was like to be here
When my existence began

I was wearing a little blue dress
With flowers all over
And my Dad, his very best
My Mother, she looked so beautiful
And so young
I would do anything to go back
And see the time that life
Wasn't so tough
For her and for me

seventeen

I walked down past the Avondale estate
Listening to Morrissey
When it was raining
And the drizzle brought out the smell
Of surrounding native trees

It reminded me of
When I would walk the streets
Of my old neighbourhood
With my mind focused in
On some bittersweet old son
My eyes glazed over in a daydream
Where anything is possible

I'd stop at the train tracks
Just before the Horsley estate
Where all the rich kids lived
And all the houses looked the same

I'd board the train alone
And stare out at the farmlands
As the train passed the escarpment into the city

I felt out of place in the centre
Where all the outcasts would wander
They were different in a way

That was electric and intriguing
And I, hopelessly awkward would ponder
That perhaps if I could be different
In a way that could make sense
I could be special like them
And party with the rest

To sit in a dingy bar
And not feel alone
Where the punks and misfits would congregate
To feel that it was my own

After school in my sunlit bedroom
I would watch old movies
And listen to the tunes
That romanticised the life
I should have been living
At seventeen

A guilt would rush through me
As I stared at my ceiling
That my life was not special
Or unique
I was not particularly beautiful
And my surrounds didn't boast a sepia sheen

My days were uneventful
And my soul even less
Even though few mistakes were made
There is much more regret

gone

I was in the middle of Crown St when I stalled
my car
I started to cry and I couldn't stop
Like this mild hiccup had been the catalyst.
It toppled down the barriers of my mental
capacity
Like nudging the top
Of a precariously stacked tower of champagne
flutes
Or glasses for my tea

I was birthed to be a fighter
A warrior, a woman
But I just don't know if I'm up to the task
anymore
My god I am just so tired
I can feel the darkness seeping through my heart
and veins
And I don't think I have the energy to fight it

The woman of strength and stature
She was taken from us last night
When fireworks lit the harbour
And we watched the clocks strike midnight

Nevertheless, i'll wake up tomorrow and prepare myself
For the one-woman show
I'll work myself to the ground
Because that's all I've ever known
You'll see me at the library, at the store, or at the office
Moving in a whirlwind
Clinging to the empty promise
That everything will be just fine

safety blanket

I don't have anything left to say
The trains of thought are stood still
I am swathed in this sadness
Like a warm, knitted blanket
Looking to that sick relief of my misery
My natural state of being
Where the pointless fancies of life fall away

The manic buzz of voices
Climbed and reached their peak
Overdrawn and weary
They bowed their heads
And went to sleep

The power and passion dripped from my skin
Those qualities, those drives that defined me
Have been stretched too far
And withered thin

Where do I go when the melancholia arrives?
In my logical state
I am aware how wrong it is to romance the
sadness
To find beauty and comfort in the mourning
For want and desire to be distant memories

To lie lifeless on my unmade bed in the later
hours of the morning
To work and to dream is what humans do
I spin in my haze of idealism and naivete
Working myself raw in the mission to prove
My worth
To live and to be happy
Maybe one day

The world is scarier than I could have ever
imagined
With lives and events ever tragic
Stacking upon each other
In a tower of unmanageable tasks
That daily life requires
Like the prospect of making my bed
Makes me break down and cry

I said "come on"
"Let's go for a drive tonight"
Where do you want to go?
I don't care, wherever is fine
Talk to me
And make the world fall away
If only for a little while

thoughts from the jewellery store floor

Lately
I've been having disturbing dreams
That make me question my sanity
What is my soul harbouring?
Deep down
Where I cannot see

There's a feeling deep in my throat
A disgusting bitter taste
I can feel a parasite
Moving its way through my body
Crawling underneath my skin

Visions of murder and violence
Lingered when I woke today
There was a body lying on my kitchen floor
In his hand a blade
I ran as fast as I could
But my god
There was no way to outrun him
And no matter what I say
No one will believe me
I've never been loved
Like this before

Among the loneliness and insanity
I knew there was always more
Waiting for me

At the age of twenty-two
When the world is so abundantly
Fruitful, yet so cruel
I am so very strong
But despite me
The past remains
She sidles just behind me

The horrors untold
They happened for a reason
Such a despicable woman
As if you deserve your freedom

You'll put on you play
And you'll pretend that you are worthy
But the sordid truth is
Your soul is tainted and dirty

teeth

He bit my bottom lip
With all the force
He could muster
Like his teeth
Were filled with all the frustration
That had been coursing through his body

There was no tracing of skin
Or delicate whispers
Only invisible bite marks
Covering my body
As time converged
On this one moment
Cruelly turning each second
Into its own eternity

I seek a safe haven
Of tender words
A meeting of minds
No teeth, no scars
Only tongues and fingertips

ode to an antidepressant

I wanted my happiness to be pure
Like my stilled, unbroken
Teenage heart
I wanted to be good enough
To live in this world on my own
Exist without falling apart

I hate myself for needing you
I hate my frail, weakened body
I hate that when I wake without you by my side
I choke, and I cry
A grey fog encapsulating my mind
My senses go numb
Blackened clouds fill the sky

I crave you like I crave a lover
Wrap yourself around my body
Slither into every part of me
Whisper in my ear
That everything will be just fine

You bring me to my knees
An artificial me
Without the natural loves and desires
That sweeten life

Like lumps of sugar into blackened tea

Give me raw emotion
Without the pain that follows
Not this gentle high that slowly simmers low
Let me move through this world
Blissfully
To elegantly flow
Like a rippling stream, curling around corners
and avoiding dips

Let his touch send waves through my body
As if he had picked up the whole ocean with one
hand
And thrown it back down again

I have died a thousand times
Since I ran from you last August
But to come back to life like this I question
Was it really worth it?

coming down

All the colours that lined my soul
Have been stripped bare
My bones ache
As the wind whips at my faded blonde hair

Does it taint my womanhood to want to be
rescued?
Like a ten-year old girl, going on twenty
Believing the knowledge
She has is plenty
To define her world

Be close to me
Touch me like i'm paper thin
Please be gentle
I'm broken underneath my skin

I have something to say
Look at me
You can see it in my eyes
You're hurting me
But i'm too damaged, too shy
To say

I don't see myself as beautiful

Or believe that I am a woman
That could be placed on a pedestal

I am feminist token
An elegant fool
To be tousled and stroked
Only before the scattering of morning dew

I see a future without love
Living my life alone
Empty hallways and a single bed
A house but not a home

Pretend that i'm yours
Just for the night
Look at me like i'm a precious deity
Like I twinkle in the moonlight

Give me something to go off
When the sunlight reappears
And i'm sitting alone on the beach
Wiping away my tears